Contents

All About Knitting

Materials....................................4

Yarns and Needles 5

Making Pom Poms......................6

Let's Knit!

Holding Your Needles 8

Casting On 9

Knit Stitch................................10

Purl Stitch.................................12

Stocking Stitch 13

Rib Stitch..................................14

Moss Stitch................................15

Changing Colours........................16

Joining Yarn 17

Increasing..................................18

Decreasing.................................19

Casting Off.................................20

Oops! Dropped Stitches................21

Sewing Together.........................22

Sewing On Buttons.......................23

Projects To Make!

Rainbow Wrist Cuffs.....................26

Pom Pom Scarf 28

Fingerless Mittens 30

Easy Hats 32

Bow Headband 34

Bunny Rabbits.............................36

Pet Couture 38

Robot Pals..................................40

Beautiful Bunting.........................42

Rabbit i-pod/phone Cover 44

All About Knitting!

Materials

As well as knitting needles and yarn, there are a few other things you will need to help you complete your projects. Why not make yourself a nice basket or box where you can keep all your knitting and sewing tools together?

Sewing Basket

When it is time to sew your projects together, you will need scissors, large tapestry or yarn needles, and some thread. You will also need a tape measure to help you measure your work, and it's always nice to have lovely buttons and things too.

Knitting Accessories

Row Counter

With some projects you may have to knit a certain number of rows. A row counter fits on the end of your needle and you can turn the dial to adjust the number at the end of each row to remind you how many you have done so far.

Needle Point Protectors

These fit over the point of your knitting needles to stop your stitches sliding off when you put your knitting down.

Stitch holders

Needle point protectors

Row counters

Stitch Holder

A stitch holder is a bit like a giant safety pin and can be used to hold your stitches together while you shape your knitting, or when you need to use the needles for another project.

Yarn and needles

Yarn (or wool) and needles are the two main things you will need when starting to knit. Here are some tips to help you choose the correct needles and yarn for your project.

Yarn!

When you start shopping for yarn, you will notice that, as well as a wonderful range of colours to choose from, it comes in all different weights or thicknesses. It's important to choose the correct thickness of yarn for the project you are making. Most projects or patterns will tell you the best weight of yarn for the job. Usually the weight or type of yarn is printed on the paper band wrapped around the ball of yarn, but if you're unsure, ask for help choosing the correct weight for your project.

When you start a project, it will tell you what size of needle and what weight of yarn to use. If you use a different thickness of yarn from what they suggest, the size of your knitting could end up completely different. Look at these examples which were knitted using the same size of needles, the same amount of stitches and rows.

Needles

Needles can be made in wood, metal or plastic, and also come in a range of sizes and thicknesses, with the size usually marked on the ends of the needles.

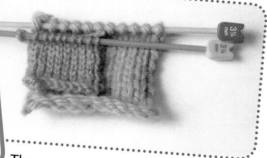

The green, thicker yarn knitted up almost **DOUBLE** the size of the lighter blue yarn.

WOW!

Needle Size Conversions

Metric	US	Old UK
4mm	6	8
4.5mm	7	7
5mm	8	6
5.5mm	9	5
7mm	$10^{1}/_{2}$	2

Making Pom Poms

Pom Poms are so fun and easy to make and can be used on all sorts of projects — on hats, scarves, bags and more! You can even make fun little creatures and toys by adding eyes and legs too! All you need is some cardboard and yarn, and some round lids or shapes to draw around, and you're all set!

1 How large would you like your pom pom? Find a jar lid, CD or something of similar size and draw around it on the cardboard. Now draw a smaller circle inside the large one (2 inches/5cm is ideal). Repeat this, so that you cut two cardboard "donuts" that are both the same.

2 If you are using a large ball of yarn, it will be too big to pass through the hole, so make a small ball that will fit by winding the yarn around your fingers lots of times. Stop before it is too large to fit through the hole.

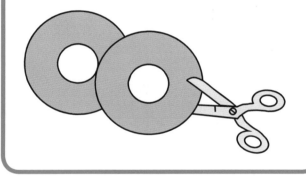

3 Now put both discs together. You're now ready to start winding your yarn around the discs.

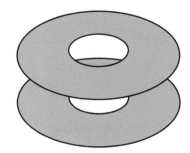

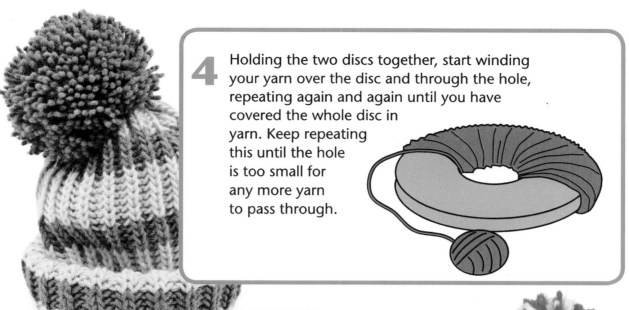

4 Holding the two discs together, start winding your yarn over the disc and through the hole, repeating again and again until you have covered the whole disc in yarn. Keep repeating this until the hole is too small for any more yarn to pass through.

5 Carefully insert one blade of your scissors between the two discs, and start cutting through the yarn. Keep moving the scissors around the edge, cutting the yarn as you go, until you have cut all the way around.

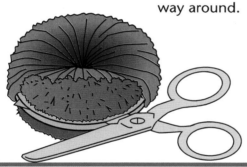

6 Cut a length of yarn and carefully pull apart the two discs slightly. Wrap your yarn between the two discs and around the middle of your pom pom, and tie in a tight knot.

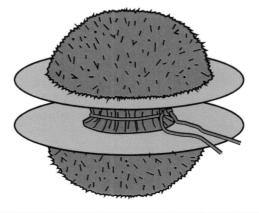

Do this a couple more times so that your pom pom is really secure. Now rip or cut each disc away, and roll your pom pom between your hands to hide the join and make it nice and fluffy!

Let's Knit!

How to Hold Your Needles

1 Once you have Cast on, you will start by holding the needle with the cast-on stitches in your left hand, and the empty needle in your right.

2 Hold the empty needle in your right hand, as though you were holding a pencil.

3 Another way to hold your right hand needle is to imagine that you are holding a knife, with your fingers close to the tip of the needle.

4 Now hold both needles and see which way is most comfortable for you. Try tucking the end of your right needle under your arm to keep it steady.

Making a Slip Knot

Before we can "Cast on" some stitches to knit, we need to start with a Slip Knot.

1 Unravel some yarn from the ball, and grip the loose end between your thumb and your hand, with your palm facing towards you.

2 Now wrap the yarn (from the ball end, not the loose end) in a loop around your first two fingers.

3 Using your right hand, reach through this loop and pull some more yarn from the ball through — this will form a new loop.

4 Hold onto this loop with your right hand, and pull gently on the loose end with your left hand. Now you're ready to slide your slip knot onto your needle!

Casting On

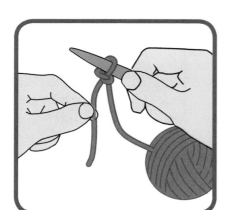

1 Slide the slip knot onto one of your needles and gently pull on the loose end to tighten it. From this point on you will always be using the ball end of the yarn, not the loose end.

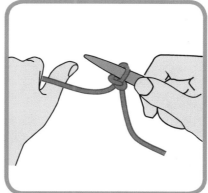

2 Holding your needle in one hand, grip the working end (the end that leads to the ball) of the yarn with the other hand.

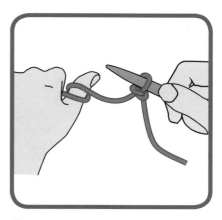

3 Wrap the yarn in a loop around your thumb.

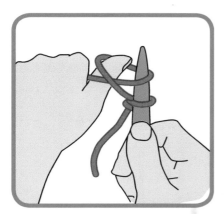

4 Push your needle tip through this loop, slide your thumb out, and pull the working end of the yarn to tighten.

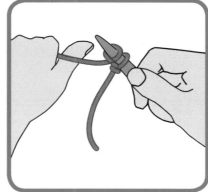

5 You have now Cast on a new stitch. Repeat Steps 2-4 until you have the correct amount of stitches that your project suggests. Why not cast on 20, ready for some practice knitting?

6 And now you have 20 stitches, ready to start KNITTING!

Let's Start Knitting!

There are two main stitches that you will use in knitting — Knit stitch and Purl stitch. These can either be knitted on their own i.e all Knit stitch or all Purl stitch, or combined in different ways to create different stitches and knitted textures.

MOSS STITCH
Moss stitch is created by alternating Knit stitch and Purl stitch...doesn't it look pretty?

KNIT STITCH
This is the first stitch you will learn when knitting. A pattern that uses all Knit stitches will look like this.

RIB STITCH
To create a ribbed effect, a combination of Knit stitch and Purl stitch is used. See page 14 for more on Rib stitch.

STOCKING STITCH
Knit one row, Purl one row, Knit one row, Purl one row...! You'll see it looks smooth on one side and bumpy on the other.

Understanding Knitting Patterns

The projects in this book are written in a very clear, easy to understand way, but once you move on to other books and knitting patterns you may find that they use certain knitting Terms or Abbreviations. Here are some of the most common:

CO = Cast On	**dec** = decrease	**inc** = Increase	**K** = Knit stitch
P = Purl stitch	**rep** = repeat	**St(s)** = Stitch(es)	**St st** = Stocking stitch

Knit Stitch

The 'working end' of the yarn is the yarn that is coming directly from the ball of yarn!

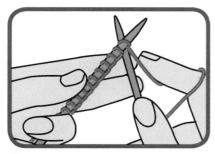

1 Hold the needle that has the cast-on stitches in your left hand, and the empty needle in your right hand. Push the point of your right hand needle up into the first stitch, from front to back.

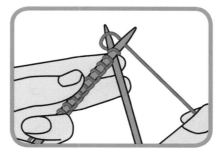

2 Now wrap the ***working end*** of the yarn around the back of the right hand needle, then around the right hand needle and between the tips of the two needles.

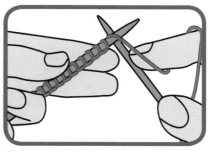

3 Holding the yarn tight, slide your right hand needle towards you, down through the stitch on the left needle.

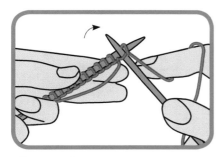

4 Slide your right hand needle up so that the stitch on the left needle slips off, and the new stitch stays on your right needle.

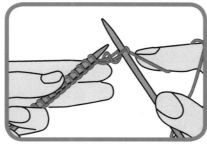

5 You will now have a loop on your right hand needle. Well done, you've just knitted a new stitch!

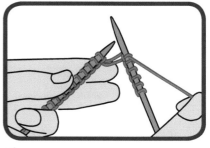

6 Pull your yarn to tighten the stitch, then repeat steps 2–6 until all the stitches from the left needle have been knitted over to your right needle.

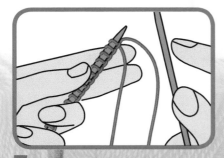

7 Now you have knitted your first ROW! Swap your needles so that the one with all the stitches is back in your left hand.

8 Keep knitting row after row and watch as your knitting grows and grows!

When we use Knit stitch for every stitch and every row, both sides will look exactly the same. This is also known as *Garter stitch*!

Purl Stitch

Purl stitch is used in combination with Knit stitch to produce various other knitting stitches and styles. On the next page, we will be using Knit stitch and Purl stitch to create Stocking stitch — so let's learn how to Purl!

1 Cast on 20 stitches using the same method as on page 9. As usual, hold the needle with the cast on stitches in your left hand, the empty needle in your right.

2 With your yarn in front of the needles, not behind, insert your right hand needle into the front of the first stitch, so that your right needle crosses over the left needle.

3 Wrap the working end of the yarn over the tip of the right needle, from right to left, so that it looks like this.

4 Slide the tip of your right needle down and away from you, pushing it through the centre of the stitch on the left needle. You will now see a loop on your right needle.

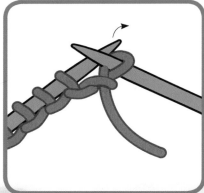

5 Keep sliding your right needle so that the original stitch slides off the left needle, but you keep the new stitch on your right needle. Well done, you've now made your first Purl stitch!

6 To Purl the whole row, repeat stages 2–5 until you have knitted all the stitches on the left needle over to the right needle.

7 If you needed to purl the next row, simply swap needles so that the needle with the stitches is in your left hand, then repeat stages 2–5 until you have purled another row…and so on.

Stocking Stitch

When we knit alternate rows of Knit stitch and Purl stitch, we create Stocking stitch. This is also sometimes called Stockinette stitch. This is a pretty stitch and looks smoother on the front side and bumpier on the back. The smooth side will look like a row of tiny "V's", and the back will look bumpier, like regular knit stitch. Let's practice Stocking stitch.

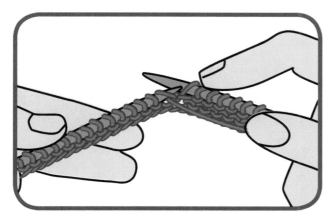

1 Cast on 20 stitches as before, and knit the whole row using Knit stitch.

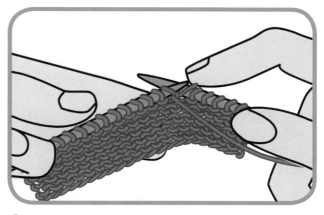

2 Bring the yarn to the front and do the next row in Purl stitch.

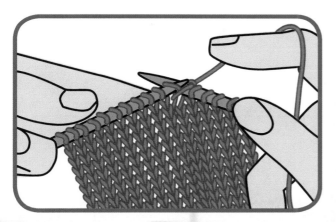

3 Keep doing alternate rows of Knit stitch, then Purl stitch. You will notice that one side of your knitting is smooth V's", and the other side is bumpy.

If you lose track of whether you knit the last row or purled it, look at your knitting. Hold your needles in the ready-to-knit position (with the left hand needle holding the stitches) and look at what's facing you. If you're looking at the smooth side, you use Knit stitch for the next row. If you're looking at the bumpy side, you purl the next row.

Easy!

Rib Stitch

Rib stitch — sometimes called Ribbing — is another cool combination of Knit stitch and Purl stitch.

Rib stitch consists of columns of Knit stitches alternating with columns of Purl stitches. To make a ribbed pattern, you change from Knit stitches to Purl stitches within a row. You should always cast on an *EVEN* number of stitches i.e. 20, 22, 28, 40 etc. when knitting Rib stitch.

To create 2x2 ribbing, cast on a multiple of 4 stitches i.e. 16, 20, 24, 28 etc. Then knit 2 stitches, purl 2 stitches, knit 2, purl 2 on each row. You can also try creating narrower or broader columns of ribbing using other combinations (always of *EVEN* numbers of stitches i.e. 1x1, 2x2, 4x4 etc.).

1 Cast on 20 stitches. Knit the first two in Knit stitch. Then bring your yarn forward between the two needles ready for Purl stitch.

2 With your yarn now in front, Purl the next two stitches. Then take the yarn back behind your needles ready for Knit stitch.

3 Continue alternating two Knit stitches, then two Purl stitches until you have reached the end of your stitches. You should have ended on two Purl stitches.

LOST TRACK OF WHAT STITCH YOU SHOULD DO NEXT? IF THE NEXT TWO STITCHES ARE *BUMPY*, YOU NEED TO PURL. IF NOT, KNIT!

4 Move the needle with the stitches on to your left hand, and begin again. Start with two Knit stitches, then two Purl stitches and so on. Don't forget to have your yarn at the *BACK* for Knit stitch, and at the *FRONT* for Purl stitch!

5 Once you have done a few rows, you will start to see the ribbed pattern!

Moss Stitch

Moss stitch is another great combination of Knit stitch and Purl stitch. Moss stitch is a pattern created by alternately working one Knit stitch and one Purl stitch on every row. The Purl stitch is then worked over the Knitted stitch on the next row.

This version is also known as Seed stitch or British Moss stitch. Row 1: K,P,K,P to end. Row 2: P,K,P,K to end. Continue to alternate each row as above.

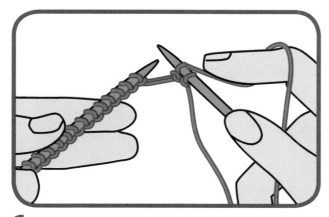

1 Cast on an *EVEN* number of stitches. Knit one stitch, then bring your yarn forward ready to purl.

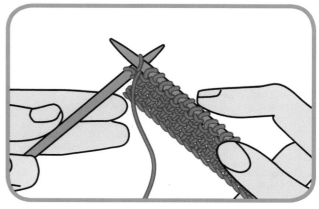

2 Carry on alternating a Knit stitch then a Purl stitch until you reach the end of the row. Because you cast on an *EVEN* number of stitches, your last stitch will be a Purl stitch. Don't forget to have your yarn at the *BACK* for Knit stitch, and at the *FRONT* for Purl stitch!

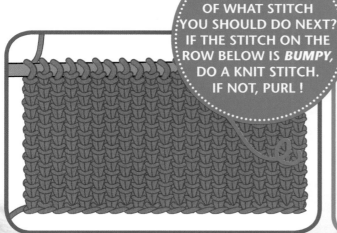

LOST TRACK OF WHAT STITCH YOU SHOULD DO NEXT? IF THE STITCH ON THE ROW BELOW IS *BUMPY*, DO A KNIT STITCH. IF NOT, PURL !

3 For your next row, start on a Purl (P) stitch, then a Knit (K) stitch, then continue to alternate each stitch with P,K,P,K to the end.

4 Continue to alternate each row so that one row begins on a Knit (K) stitch, the next begins on a Purl (P) stitch — and you alternate the Knit and Purl stitches within the row.

Changing Colours

Using a single colour of yarn is fine for your first projects, but after a while you could try something a little more interesting. A fun and easy technique for adding interest to your knitted items is adding stripes.

Stripes are simple, but you need to know a few things before you get started. The main thing you need to know when knitting in stripes is where to change colours. Remember to change colours at the end of a row so that your stripes will be nice and even. When you knit something with narrow stripes, rather than cut the yarn each time you change colour, you can "carry" the yarn up the side of your knitting until you are ready to use that colour again. Here's how:

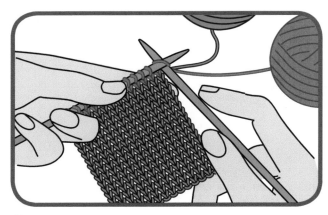

1 When you have finished an even number of rows (2, 4, 6 etc. — your pattern should tell you how many), leave the ball attached and just start knitting with the next colour. To add the new colour, leave a few inches of tail, hold it tight as you would hold the yarn to begin a regular row, and begin knitting.

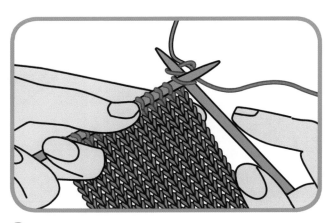

2 The next time you get to that side (which would be after 2 rows, but it could even be after 4, 6, 8 or more even rows, depending on your pattern) pick up the old colour, wrap the yarn you're working with around it and go on knitting with the old colour. This will secure the yarn to the side of the project and move it up to where you'll need it next.

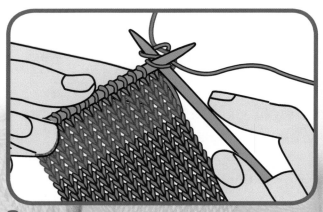

3 Repeat this process for each new stripe, so that the yarn is carried up the side each time.

4 Hurrah, you've made some stripes!

Joining Yarn

At some point during a project you may find that you will soon run out of yarn — you've used the whole ball — so you need to start using a fresh ball of the same yarn. To do this you need to "join" your yarn. Here's how:

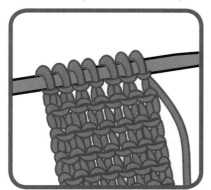

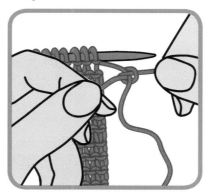

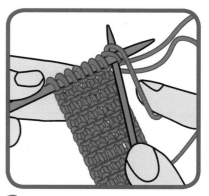

1 You should always aim to join your yarn at the end of a row, not in the middle. So finish the row you are working on, and leave at least 6 inches/15cm of yarn from the first ball. You will need this much to tie it onto the new ball.

2 Using a loose knot, tie the old yarn to the end of the new ball, making your knot as close to the edge of your knitting as possible.

3 Now you can start using the new ball of yarn to knit with. Don't worry about the loose end from the old yarn, here's how you can sew in this loose end once you have finished the knitting.

Sewing in Loose Ends

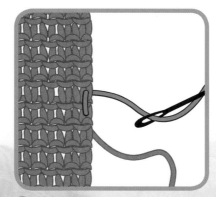

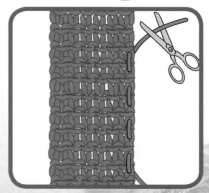

1 Use a needle with a large enough eye for your loose yarn to be threaded through. Thread the needle with the loose yarn, and sew one stitch to the row above, close to the edge of the knitting.

2 Pull the yarn through, then make a new stitch into the row above, close to the edge again.

3 Keep stitching like this until you have either done 6 stitches, or your yarn has run out. After 6 stitches, cut the end from the yarn as it is now secure enough. Be VERY careful not to cut into your knitting accidentally!

# Increasing

Increasing the number of stitches is a way to either make your knitting wider, or to create shapes in your knitting. There are a couple of ways to do this, and which way to increase will depend on the shape you are making and what the pattern tells you to do.

Increasing at the beginning of a row

This is sometimes also called a **Cable Increase** and can be used to add one or more extra stitches at the beginning of a row.

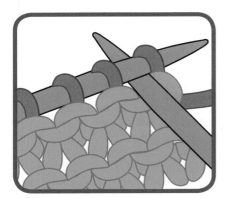

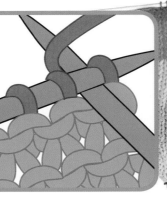

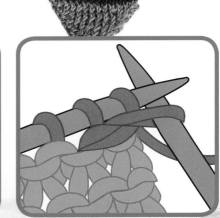

1 Slip the tip of your right needle in between the first two stitches of the left needle.

2 Wrap the working end of the yarn under and around the right needle. Hold the yarn tight.

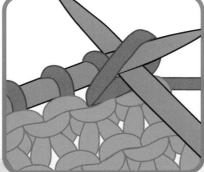

3 Now draw the right needle towards you, pulling it through and under the two stitches on the left needle. You will now have a new loop on your right needle.

4 Now slide this new loop onto your left needle, at the end. You have now increased by one stitch.

5 If your pattern tells you to add more than one stitch at this point, do so, then continue knitting as normal.

Increasing anywhere in a row

This is also called a **Bar increase** and is good for adding a single extra stitch anywhere within a row. You can only add one extra stitch at a time using this method.

1 Knit a stitch as usual, but do not slide the stitch off the left hand needle like you would usually.

2 Now slip your right needle into the *BACK* of this same stitch on your left needle.

3 Knit this stitch again. You will now have two more stitches on your right needle.

4 Now you can slip the original stitch off the left needle like you would usually. You have now increased your knitting by one extra stitch.

 # Decreasing

By decreasing the number of stitches, you can make your knitting narrower. Decreasing removes stitches, narrowing the knitting.

Decrease Method 1: Knitting 2 Together

This method of decreasing can be used anywhere in a row — at the beginning, middle or end. You can decrease by just one stitch each time this way. Slip your right needle into two stitches on your left needle, instead of one. Knit them both together as though they were just one stitch. You have now decreased by one stitch and can continue knitting according to your pattern.

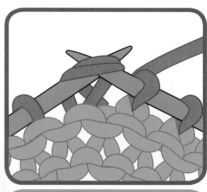

Decrease Method 2: Casting-off

This method can be used to decrease stitches at the beginning or end of a row, not in the middle. It uses the same technique as Casting off at the very end of your knitting — turn over to page 20 for more details. You would follow Step 1 and Step 2 for each stitch you needed to decrease by.

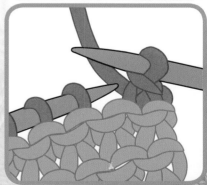

Casting Off

Once you have finished a piece of knitting you need to secure the stitches and ends of your yarn so that it does not unravel. This is done by using a method called **Casting Off**.

1 Knit two stitches, then slide the tip of your left needle into the front of the first stitch you knitted onto your right needle.

2 Now carefully lift that first stitch over the second stitch, and slip it off the tip of the right needle. Pull your yarn tight.

3 Slide out your left needle, and now you will have just one stitch left on the right needle. Now knit over one more stitch from the left needle onto the right, so that you have 2 stitches on the right needle again.

4 Repeat Step 2, slipping the first stitch over the second stitch and off the right needle. Keep knitting a second stitch onto the right needle, and reducing it to one using Step 2. You should only ever have 2 stitches at a time on the right needle, ready to reduce to one stitch.

5 Keep doing this until you are left with just one stitch on your left needle.

6 Cut the yarn, leaving about 6 inches/15cm and pull the end of the yarn through the final stitch (it may help to pull the left needle away so that the stitch becomes a larger loop). Pull tightly, and your knitting has now been safely cast off and secured!

Dropped Stitches

When you first start knitting, it's easy to accidentally drop the odd stitch. If this happens, don't worry, it's pretty easy to fix!

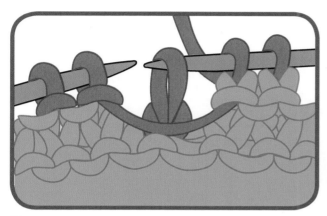

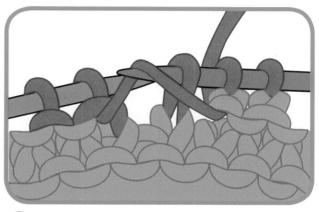

1 Can you see where the dropped stitch has slipped to? Catch it with the tip of your right needle, slipping the needle tip through the stitch.

2 Now can you see a loose strand of yarn which should have been part of your new stitch. Slip the tip of your right needle under this too.

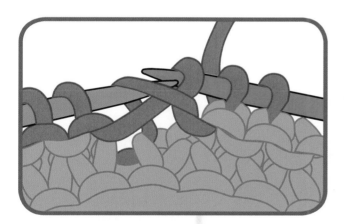

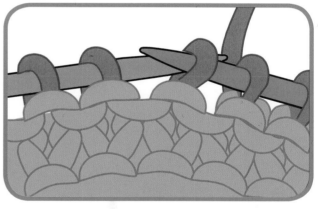

3 Now you will need your left needle to help with the job! Use the tip of the left needle to slip under the dropped stitch (which is now on your right needle) and pull it over the strand that you also caught, then let it drop off the right needle. A lot like when you Bind-off or Cast off. You now have the proper stitch on your right needle.

4 But this stitch actually needs to be on your left needle so that you can "knit" it properly. So use your left needle to help slide it over onto the left needle. Now you have "caught" the dropped stitch and it is ready to be knitted as normal. Hurrah!

Sewing Together

Once you have knitted all the parts of a project, it will be time to sew them together. Usually you will want your stitches to be hidden, so you should use a large needle and the same yarn to sew the pieces together.

You may already know some sewing stitches, but here's a new one used especially in knitting — **Mattress stitch**. This stitch is a great way to sew together knitted pieces as invisibly as possible. When sewing knitting together, always use a large tapestry needle (make sure your tapestry needle is blunt to avoid piercing the yarn).

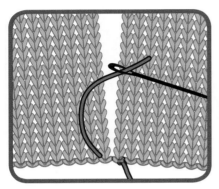

1 Lay the pieces you wish to join on a flat surface, side by side, with the right side (the outside) facing up. Use a length of the same yarn, and thread your needle, then secure it to the end of your knitted work with a couple of stitches on top of each other. OR if you left a tail of yarn, use this if it is long enough).

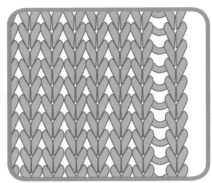

2 Now, look closely at the knitting and gently pull apart the first two edge stitches. Can you see the series of little horizontal running threads connecting them? We will be using these for our mattress stitches.

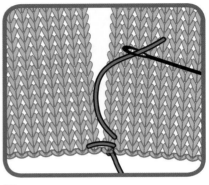

3 Put your needle under and through the horizontal running thread that runs between the first and second stitch on the opposite piece of knitting, like in this diagram. Pull your yarn all the way through.

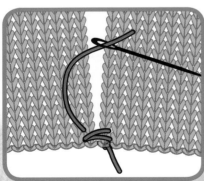

4 Cross over to the other piece of knitting and do the same, on the same stitch, on that side. Pull the yarn through again. Carry on like this, zig zagging from one piece to the other, moving up one stitch each time.

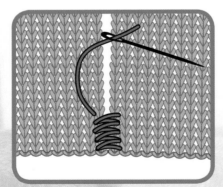

5 Each time you make a stitch and pull on the yarn tight, you will be creating a strong "seam" to hold your work together. When you reach the end, secure with 2 or 3 stitches on top of each other.

THE *RIGHT SIDE* IS THE SIDE OF YOUR KNITTED PIECE THAT YOU WANT ON DISPLAY. THE *WRONG SIDE* WILL BE THE BACK, OR THE INSIDE, OF YOUR KNITTED ITEM.

Sewing On Buttons

Once you have knitted something, you may want to add buttons to look like eyes, or just to make it prettier. Sewing on buttons is easy when you know how!

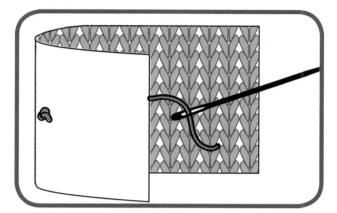

1 Thread your needle with matching yarn or thread and tie a knot at the far end. (Before doing this, double check that the eye of your needle fits through the holes in your button! If not, use a smaller needle!) Decide where you want your button to be, and bring your needle up through the middle of that area, from the rear of the knitting so that the needle comes out on the RIGHT side.

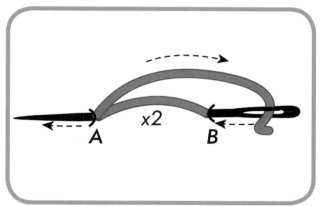

2 Now sew two small stitches on top of each other. This will secure your thread or yarn to the knitting before you start sewing on your button.

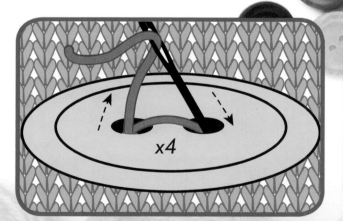

3 Grab your button and place it over the area it will go. Now bring your needle and thread up through one hole of the button. Pull thread all the way. Next go down through the other hole, again pulling thread all the way. Do this 4 times, or until it no longer feels wobbly when you tug on it.

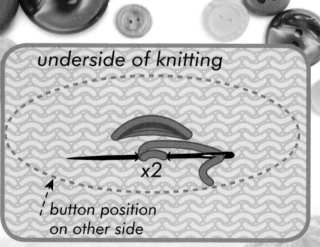

underside of knitting

button position
on other side

4 On the underside of the knitting, just underneath where the button now is, do two or three small stitches to secure your thread or yarn. You have now sewn on your button and can cut the extra yarn off. *Be VERY careful not to cut into your knitting!*

PROJECTS

Now that you have practiced your knitting stitches, it's time to make some cool projects! What will you make first?

Rainbow Wrist Cuffs

by Alison McNicol

These wrist cuffs are so easy to knit, and a great way to use up small amounts of leftover yarn. You can make them in all sorts of thicknesses, sizes and colour combinations, and decorate them with cool buttons and trims. Why not make these as friendship bracelets for all of your friends?

You Will Need:

1 pair of 4.5mm knitting needles

Double knitting yarn, in various rainbow colours

Buttons to decorate, if you like

How to Knit Rainbow Wrist Cuffs:

These are knitted in Stocking stitch (St st) to give a cool, smooth appearance.
Decide which order you would like to knit your colours in before you start knitting.

Cast on 20 stitches with *Colour 1*.

Knit (K) stitch the first row.

Purl (P) the next row.

Repeat. You have now done 4 rows in *Colour 1*.

Change yarn to *Colour 2* (see page 16) and do the same — Knit a row, Purl a row, Knit a row, Purl a row.

Now change to *Colour 3* and do the same Stocking Stitch (Knit a row, Purl a row) for the next 4 rows.

Then change to yarn *Colour 4* and do the same for the next 4 rows (Knit a row, Purl a row).

Cast off. Leave a tail of yarn approx. 6 inches/15cm for sewing up.

Making up Rainbow Wrist Cuffs:

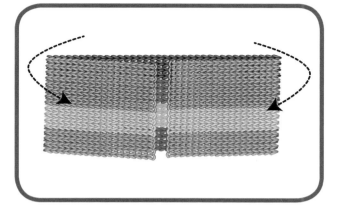

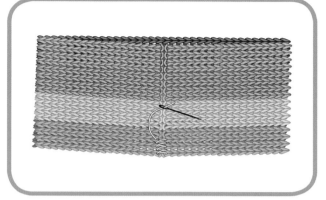

1 Place your knitted piece right sides up (that's the nice side that will be the outside of your cuff) and bring each short end in into the middle to meet each other.

2 Thread your needle with the tail of yarn and use mattress stitch (page 22) to sew the ends together. Don't forget to start with a few stitches together at the start and end. Hurrah! — your Rainbow Wristband is now ready to wear!

You can also knit up cool cuffs in just one colour, and try out various stitches and sizes. For a one-colour band like this, Cast on just 5 stitches, then knit until it is long enough to fit around your wrist. Sew up and add on buttons.

Pom Pom Scarf

by Sandra Fardon Fox

To make a stripy scarf like the one in the picture, you will need three colours — a light one, a medium one and a dark one will give a good effect. A scarf is so easy to make and can just as easily be knitted with more or less stripes. OR for something REALLY easy, knit it all in just one colour.

You Will Need:

1 pair of 7mm needles

Chunky weight yarn (200g for a single colour, or for stripes 100g of each colour). Acrylic is a good choice because it's machine washable

Tapestry needle for sewing up

How to Knit a Pom Pom Scarf

This particular scarf was knitted using Knit stitch for the whole scarf, but once you have more experience you can try knitting scarves in all sorts of stitches!

Start with your medium colour (*yarn A*).

Cast on 16 stitches (leave a tail of approx. 10 inches/25cm).

Knit (K) your first 2 rows in Knit stitch.

Change to your light colour (*yarn B*), knit (K) 2 more rows in Knit stitch.*

Change to your dark colour (*yarn C*), knit (K) 2 rows.

Continue as above — Knitting 2 rows in each colour — until your scarf measures around 55 inches/140cm, or longer if you prefer.

Keep knitting in each colour until you are back on *yarn A* as you want to finish off with this.

After you have knit the last 2 rows in *yarn A*, cast off all stitches leaving a long tail of yarn of approx. 10 inches/25cm. (See page 20 again to remind you how to cast off.)

> ### *KNITTING TIP!
> *See page 16 to remind yourself how to change yarn colours. To create the lovely 'barber shop swirl' up one side of your scarf, carry your yarn up the side as you work by twisting the colour you're about to work with over the others. Remember to always twist in the same direction to keep your yarn tidy, otherwise you'll end up with knitting spaghetti!*

Making up the Pom Pom Scarf:

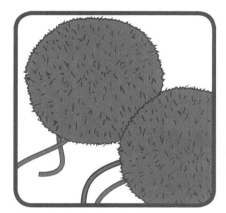

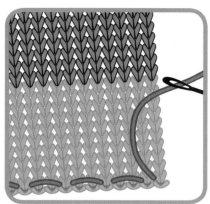

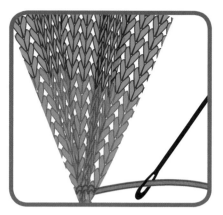

1 Make two pom poms of 4 inches/10cm diameter (see page 6), and leave the ends of the yarn you used to secure round the middle (approx. 6 inches/15cm long) to make it easy to attach to your scarf.

2 Now grab the long tail of yarn you left at one end of your scarf and thread it with a large tapestry needle. Sew a running stitch along the short end of your scarf. When you reach the other end, pull it tight so it gathers up neatly.

3 Sew a couple of knots to keep the gathers in place by pushing your needle through the middle of the bunch of gathers and then passing your needle through the loop before you pull it tight. Cut the yarn close to the edge of the scarf and unthread your needle.

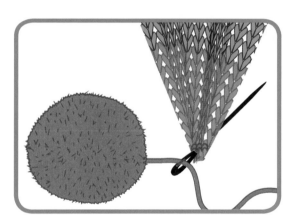

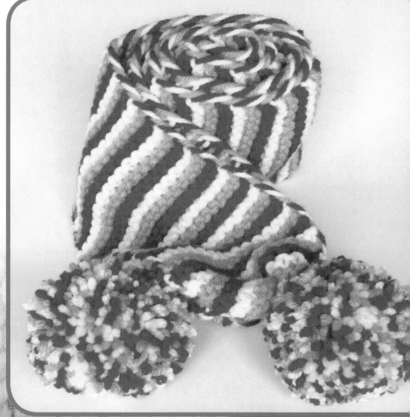

4 Now thread your needle using one of the tails of yarn that is attached to your pom pom. Use this to sew the pom pom tightly on to the end of your scarf. Once secure, cut and do the same for the other end of your scarf.

Fingerless Mittens

by Katy Penman

These gorgeous mittens are so easy to knit and can be adapted in all sorts of ways. They can be knitted in pretty much any stitch you like — how about Stocking stitch or Moss stitch? — and you could even create cool stripy ones with leftover yarn.

For your first pair, let's use a simple Knit stitch, and one colour of yarn, to help you get the hang of it!

You Will Need:

1 pair of 4.5 mm knitting needles

Aran weight yarn
(approx. 60g per pair of mittens)

Buttons, bows or fabric/wool flowers to decorate

How to Knit Fingerless Mittens:

Cast on 40 stitches.

Knit (K) stitch each row until your work measures 6 inches/15cm.

Cast off, leaving a short tail around 4 inches/10cm long.

You will now have one knitted rectangle, which will make a mitten.
Do the same again to create a second rectangle.

How about adding felt appliqué flowers or shapes to your gloves? A quick tip is that it's easier to sew your felt shapes on before you make up the gloves, but be careful to place your appliqués so that your gloves are a mirror image of each other, and your design ends up on the back of each hand.

Making up Fingerless Mittens:

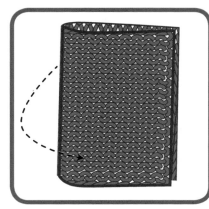  

1 Lay your knitted rectangle with the wrong side (the inside) facing up, and the Cast On and Cast off edges running across the top and bottom of rectangle. Grab the left edge and fold in half, lengthways. Now place your hand on top.

2 Notice where your thumb sticks out — this will be where you need to leave a hole in your joining up. You can mark where to stop sewing by putting safety pins at the top and bottom of the hole. You can now use the 4 inches/10cm tail you left to sew the top section.

DO NOT STITCH

3 Now sew the sides up using mattress stitch (see page 22), remembering that gap for your thumb! Don't forget to secure the stitches with 2 or 3 stitches on top of each other at the beginning and the end of each section you sew, otherwise your mittens will burst apart when you wear them!

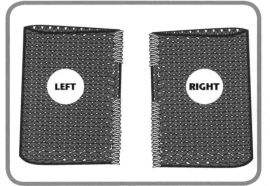

LEFT RIGHT

4 Repeat the process with your other glove, but remember to measure against the other hand and set the thumb hole in the same location. Now your mittens are ready to wear!

Easy Hats

by Ashley Holdsworth

Baby it's cold outside…time for a nice cosy hat to keep the winter chills at bay!

These cute hats are very easy to knit, and are just a simple rectangle shape which we then fold and sew up. We will be using a Knit (K) stitch for every stitch and every row. This is called Garter stitch.

Because the hats are very stretchy, the instructions below will make a hat that fits anyone from 6 to 106! You could also try making a little matching hat for your favourite teddy or doll!

You will need:

1 pair of 4.5mm knitting needles

3 colours of double knitting (DK yarn). One full ball makes 1 hat so you'll need 3 x 1/3 balls for a 3 colour hat

Piece of card for pom pom

How to knit Easy Hats:

These hats are knit side-to-side rather than up and down. This hat uses 3 colours — perhaps you could knit one to match the Pom Pom Scarf?

Start off with *colour 1*, Cast on 50 stitches.

Knit (K) stitch the first 2 rows.

Change yarn to *colour 2* (see page 16), knit (K) stitch 2 more rows.

Change yarn to *colour 3*, knit (K) stitch 2 more rows.

Carry on knitting, changing colour after every 2 rows as before.

Keep knitting until the length of your piece of knitting will go all the way around your head (the stripes should go up and down, not side to side). This could be between 40cm-50cm, depending on how old you are, the size of your head and the thickness of your hair.

When your knitting will go all the way around your head, Cast off.

If you prefer, you can use one or two colours — you could even make a hat in the colours of your school or favourite football team!

Making up Easy Hats:

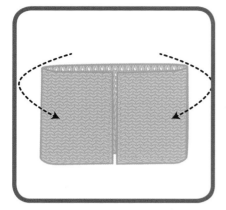

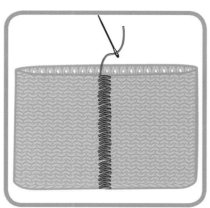

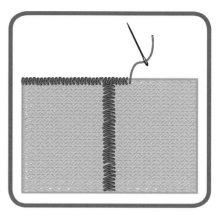

1 Lay your rectangle of knitting wrong side facing up (that's the side that will become the inside of the hat), and with the stripes running up and down. Fold the two outside edges in to the middle to meet each other.

2 Now use mattress stitch (see page 22) to sew these two edges together (be careful not to stitch into the back of the hat!) This will make a tube.

3 Now lay the tube flat, with the stitched seam down the middle. Now sew the top two edges together.

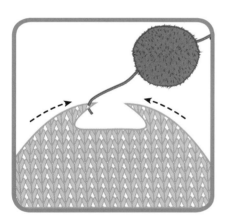

4 The hat will look square when it's flat on the table, but when you put it on, it will look like it has pointy 'ears'! If you like, make a pom pom and pull each ear into the middle and stitch the pom pom in place.

Teddy Size Hat
To make a smaller hat for a teddy or doll, do the same as above but Cast on just 25 stitches, and knit until it fits around their head. Then sew up and, if you like, add a pom pom to match yours!

Bow Headband

by Alison McNicol

These pretty headbands can be knitted up in no time and are super easy to make. Why not make one to match each outfit? You could knit the headband and bow in 2 different colours, like I have here, to make the bow really "pop"!

You Will Need:

1 pair of 7mm knitting needles

Chunky yarn in 1 or 2 matching colours (approx. 40g for headband and 10g for bow)

How to Knit Your Bow Headband:

To create a nice smooth effect, we will use Stocking stitch (St st).

Cast on 10 stitches.

Knit your first row in Knit (K) stitch.

Then the second row in Purl (P) stitch.

Then continue knitting rows, alternating between a row of Knit (K) stitch and a row of Purl (P) stitch.

When you have knitted a piece around 16 inches/40 cm long, wrap it around your head, as though it were a headband, to see if it is long enough yet.

If not, keep knitting until the length you have knitted fits exactly around your head, in the position you would wear your headband.

TIP: Slide your stitches down to the far end of the needle while you do this — or use a needle point protector if you have one — this will stop your knitting accidentally slipping off your needle!

Once you have the perfect length, Cast off.

How to Knit the Bow:

Are you using a different colour yarn for the bow?

Cast on 10 stitches.

Knit in Stocking stitch (St st) as before, until you have knitted around 5 inches/13cm. (To see how this would look as a bow, pinch this piece of knitting in the middle. Do a few more rows until it is the size you want).

Cast off.

For the middle part of the bow, Cast on 5 stitches.

Knit, using Stocking stitch (St st) until you have knitted around 4 inches/10cm. Cast off.

Making up Your Bow Headband:

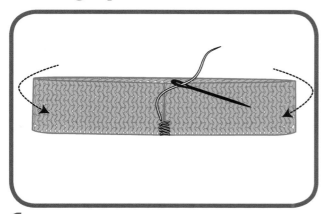

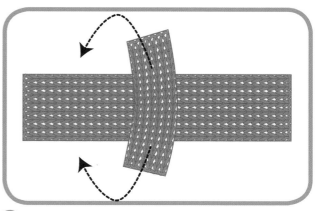

1 Lay the large piece of knitting that will be your headband with the wrong side facing up. Now fold each short end until they meet in the middle, then use mattress stitch to sew the ends together. You now have a plain headband, ready for your bow.

2 Now take the two smaller pieces that will become the bow. Lay the larger piece right sides up. Take the smaller piece and wrap it around the middle, again with the right side facing you.

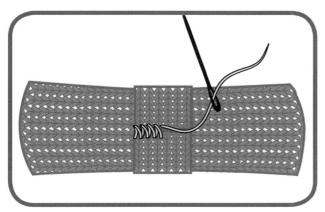

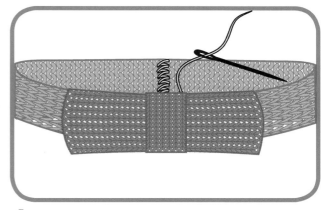

3 Now flip the bow over, and you will see where the ends of the smaller piece meet. Sew this securely. You now have a lovely bow! Take your headband so that the join is at the back and position your bow at the front, near the middle.

4 To sew the bow onto the headband, start by securing a few stitches on the headband, then stitch through the back of the bow, then onto the headband, the repeat until your bow feels secure. All your stitching should be hidden beneath the bow. Finish with a few more stitches on the headband to secure.

Here we have used chunky rainbow yarn which has various colours worked through it, so that it knits up to create a really cool multi-colour effect!

Bunny Rabbits

by Addy Whitfield

These little rabbits make great friends…and what's more they don't eat much or leave a mess! You can make them in whatever colour you like, and even knit a whole rabbit family and give them names!

You Will Need:

1 pair of 4.5mm knitting needles, plus 1 extra 4.5mm needle

1 ball of chunky yarn

Black felt for eyes and nose, cute button, needle and thread

Handful of toy filling

How to Knit a Bunny Rabbit:

This bunny is knitted in Stocking (St st) stitch — alternate rows of Knit (K) stitch and Purl (P) stitch.

Cast on 20 stitches.

Start off with a row in Knit (K) stitch.

Then bring yarn forward and knit a row in Purl (P) stitch.

Keep going, alternating a Knit (K) row with a Purl (P) row, until you have done a total of 30 rows.

NOW — Knit (K) stitch just 10 of your stitches and stop. In order to "split" the knitting to make ears, we're only going to work on JUST those 10 stitches for now. Place a needle end protector over the other needle to stop those stitches slipping off while you work on the first 10 stitches only. Now grab your spare 4.5mm needle and we can start working on the first 10 stitches.

Purl a row, then Knit a row, then keep alternating until you have knit 15 rows altogether. You should end on a Purl row. Now Cast off. You have now made the first bunny ear!

Now let's go back to those other 10 stitches on the other needle.

We need to re-attach the end of the ball of yarn to these stitches so that we can knit them. Slip the end of the yarn through the first stitch and tie a knot.

Now, start with a Knit (K) row, Stocking stitch (Knit a row, Purl a row) 16 rows in total. Then Cast off.

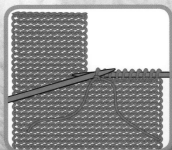

Hurrah — you have now knitted one side of your bunny. Do the exact same thing again to knit a second side.

How to Make up Your Bunny Rabbit:

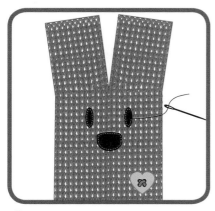

1 It is easiest to sew on the eyes, nose and button before we sew the two sides together, so cut them out from black felt and stitch on to the right side of one of the bunny pieces (side 1).

2 Lay side 1 facing up again, and place the other bunny piece (side 2) on top, so that the right sides (what will become the outside of the bunny) are touching. This means you should be looking at the wrong side, the bumpy side, of side 2.

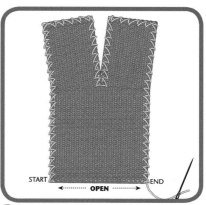

3 Now, using mattress stitch (see page 22) sew the two sides together, leaving the bottom section of the bunny open. Remember to secure three stitches on top of each other at the start and end.

4 Now turn your bunny the right way out, and fill with toy filling, pushing right up into his ears. Once full, stitch the bottom closed securely. To make his ears, tightly tie a piece of yarn around the base and knot securely.

Why not add a button or pom pom to make a cute tail for your bunny?

Pet Couture

by Alison McNicol

Fluffy fashions for your favourite friends!

When winter strikes, it's not just humans who like to wrap up warm and cosy! If you've already knitted a nice scarf or hat for yourself, why not try a matching one for your favourite pet? These cute accessories take no time at all to knit, and are a great way to try out new stitches or use up leftover yarn.

You Will Need:

1 pair of 4.5mm knitting needles

Various colours of double knitting yarn (DK yarn) — this will be stretchy when knitted

Piece of card for pom poms

Tapestry needle

How to Knit a Cat or Doggy-sized Scarf

The width and length of your scarf will depend on what size your pet is.

For a cat or small dog — Cast on 10 stitches

For a larger dog — Cast on 15 or 20 stitches.

Keep knitting, in whatever stitch you like, until the scarf is just long enough to wrap around your pet.

Cast off.

You can now add pom poms (see page 6) if you like!

> ### SAFETY FIRST
> *Always keep a close eye on your pet when wearing as the scarf could become caught or tangled and present a choking hazard.*

How to Knit a Cat or Doggy-sized Hat

To knit a smaller pet-sized hat, we simply follow the instructions for a regular **Easy Hat** (see page 32), but cast on less stitches and knit less rows.

For a cat or small dog — Cast on 20 stitches.

For a larger dog — Cast on 30 stitches.

Then knit row after row until it fits around their head.

Then sew up and, if you like, add a pom pom to match yours!

POM POMS

Make sure you sew these on VERY securely as they can easily come loose when pets play with them!

Robot Pals

by Addy Whitfield

You Will Need:

1 pair of 4.5mm knitting needles, plus 1 spare 4.5mm needle

1 ball of chunky yarn in 2 colours (2 balls total)

Black yarn for eyes and mouth, pink felt for control panel and nose, large buttons for ears, pretty buttons for controls

Tapestry needle and thread

How to Knit a Stripy Robot:

If you'd like a stripy robot, follow these instructions. If you'd prefer him to be all one colour, simply skip the parts where you are asked to change yarn colour. These little guys are knitted in Stocking Stitch (Knit a row, then Purl a row).

Robot Body (Make 2)

We will begin knitting at his head:

Cast on 9 stitches in *Colour 1*.

Knit (K) stitch a row, Purl (P) a row, K a row, P a row (4 rows total).

Change yarn to *Colour 2*.

Stocking stitch 4 more rows. Change back to *Colour 1*.

Stocking stitch (K,P) 2 rows.

Shaping the shoulders:

Next row: Before you begin knitting, cast on 3 extra stitches, so that you now have 12 on the needle. Knit (K) stitch these 12 stitches.

Next row: Start by casting on 3 extra stitches, so that you now have 15 on the needle. Purl (P) this row to the end.

Change yarn to *Colour 2*. Stocking stitch 4 rows.

Change yarn to *Colour 1*. Stocking stitch 4 rows.

Change yarn to *Colour 2*. Stocking stitch 4 rows.

Change yarn to *Colour 1*. Stocking stitch 4 rows.

Change yarn to *Colour 2*. Stocking stitch 2 rows.

Shaping the feet:

Now we need to divide our 15 stitches into two sets of 6 stitches, with a gap in the middle. This will allow us to knit individual feet.

Knit 7 stitches, cast off 3 stitches, knit the remaining 5 stitches.

You will now have a total of 12 stitches on your needle, 6, then a gap then 6 more.

Just like we did with the ears for the Bunny Rabbits (page 36), we now need to use our spare knitting needle, so we can work on the sets of 6 stitches separately. Using the spare needle:

Purl the first 6 stitches. Now pop a needle protector on the end of the needle that holds the remaining 6. We'll come back to these later.

Change yarn to *Colour 1*. Stocking Stitch 4 rows. Cast off.

To make the other foot, we will now work on the other 6 stitches.

Re-join the *Colour 2* yarn to the first stitch.

Purl (P) one row, then change yarn to *Colour 1*. Stocking stitch 4 rows. Cast off.

Well done, you have now knitted one side of your robot. Repeat to knit the second side!

Arms (Make 2):

Starting at the hand, Cast on 10 stitches in *Colour 2*.

Beginning with a Knit (K) row, Stocking stitch 4 rows. Change yarn to *Colour 1*.

Starting with a Knit (K) row, Stocking stitch 12 rows.

Cast off, leaving a small tail of yarn for sewing up.

Making up Robot Pals:

Well done, you have now knitted a front and back panel, and two arms. It's time to turn these into a robot!

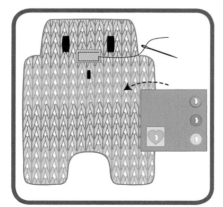

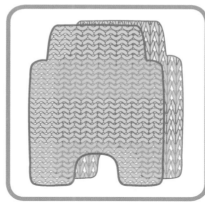

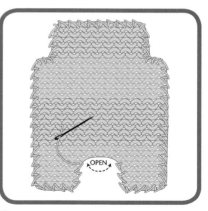

1 It is easiest to sew on the eyes, nose and control panel before we sew the two sides together, so first use the black yarn to sew some eyes and a mouth onto the front panel of the robot. (Sew on to the right side, which is the smooth side of the knitting). Next cut a nose shape from pink felt and stitch in place. Sew your buttons and shapes on to a square of felt, just like in the picture, then sew this "control" panel on to your robot body!

2 Lay this piece facing up, then place the other robot body piece (side 2) on top, so that the right sides (what will become the outside of the robot) are touching. This means you should be looking at the wrong side, the bumpy side, of side 2.

3 Now, using mattress stitch (see page 22) sew the two sides together, leaving the section between the legs of the robot open for stuffing. Turn the right way round and stuff, then sew up the gap.

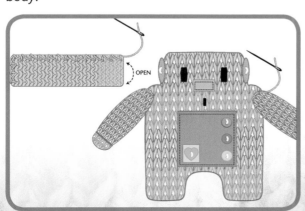

4 **Arms:** Fold each arm in half, longways, so that the side seams meet. Starting at the hand end, sew the seams together, around the hand and along the long edge. Leave the far end open, turn right side out, then stuff. Sew up the open end of the hand before sewing the arm on to the robot. Now stitch on large buttons for his ears.

Beautiful Bunting

by Jenny McHardy

This pretty bunting looks great in any bedroom or nursery, or even draped across a fireplace. To make a string of bunting we will need lots of triangles — some small and some large. Before you begin, why not look at page 19 again to remind yourself how to Decrease stitches. We'll be using Method 1: Knitting 2 Together, also shown as k2tog.

You Will Need:

1 pair of 4.5mm knitting needles
1 ball of aran yarn in 3 colours (3 balls total)
Yarn or ribbon to join the bunting
Tapestry needle and thread, and pins

How to Knit the Bunting:

We used 10 triangles here, but your bunting could be longer or shorter — it's up to you! Each triangle uses only Knit (K) stitch for each stitch and each row — as you know, this is called Garter stitch.

Large triangles
(Make 3 in colour 1 and 3 in colour 2)

Cast on 21 stitches.

Knit (K) stitch 4 rows.

 # **Knit 2 stitches together (k2tog) at the beginning of the row, then knit as normal until you get to the last 2 stitches, then knit these 2 together (k2tog).**

Then knit 2 more rows as normal #.

Repeat these 3 rows from # to # (decreasing at the beginning and end of row 1, knit as normal for rows 2 and 3) until you have just 3 stitches left.

Knit (K) stitch 2 more rows.

Knit first 2 stitches together, knit remaining stitch as normal.

Now Cast off using last 2 stitches and cut the end of the yarn, leaving a short tail. Slip this through the final stitch and pull to tighten.

Sew in end neatly.

Small triangles
(Make 4 in colour 3)

Cast on 11 stitches.

Knit (K) stitch 4 rows.

 # **Knit 2 stitches together (k2tog) at the beginning of the row, then knit as normal until you get to the last 2 stitches, then knit these 2 together (k2tog).**

Then knit 2 more rows as normal #.

Repeat these 3 rows from # to # (decreasing at the beginning and end of row 1, knit as normal for rows 2 and 3) until you have just 3 stitches left.

Knit (K) stitch 2 more rows.

Knit first 2 stitches together, knit remaining stitch as normal.

Now Cast off using last 2 stitches and cut the end of the yarn, leaving a short tail. Slip this through the final stitch and pull to tighten.

Sew in end neatly.

Making up Beautiful Bunting:

Well done, you now have at least 10 lovely knitted triangles. It's time to turn these into bunting! If you know how to finger knit, you could make a chain using spare yarn **OR** Cast on just 2 stitches and knit a long chain in matching yarn. If you don't fancy either of these methods, you can always use a length of ribbon that matches your triangles.

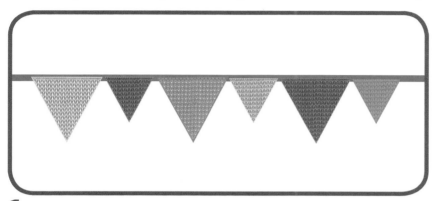

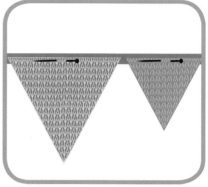

1 Lay out your ribbon or knitted length, and position your triangles on top so that they are evenly spaced and the colours alternate.

2 Now pin each triangle in place so they stay evenly spaced.

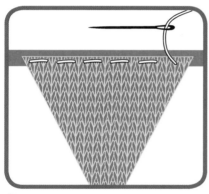

3 Use your needle and thread to sew each triangle on to the ribbon or yarn chain. Remember to begin and end with a knot and a double stitch so you sew each one on securely.

4 You could even personalise it by cutting letters from felt and sewing your name onto the bunting!

Rabbit i-Pod/Phone Cover

by Jenny McHardy

This cute little fella will keep your phone or i-pod nice and cosy and safe, *AND* he uses very little yarn so can be made from leftover yarn in whatever colours you have to hand!

You Will Need:

1 pair of 4.5mm knitting needles

Aran weight yarn, cream, lilac, green, blue and a tiny bit of black for the eyes

Tapestry needle for sewing up

How to Knit Mr Rabbit:

Body

With blue yarn cast on 28 stitches.

Knit your first 2 rows in Knit (K) stitch.

Change to lilac yarn, then Knit (K) stitch 2 rows.

Change to green yarn, Knit (K) stitch 2 rows.

Repeat these 6 rows once more: Knit (K) 2 rows in blue, 2 rows lilac, 2 rows green.

Then Knit (K) 2 rows in blue, then 2 rows lilac.

NOW **change to cream yarn for the main body of the rabbit.**

Knit (K) a row all the way to the end.

Purl (P) the next row.

Now continue to knit (K) a row, then purl (P) a row — so you are doing Stocking stitch, see page 13 — until you have knitted a total of 17 rows in the cream yarn.

Your 17th row should be Knit (K) stitch.

Knit (K) stitch for the next 5 rows.

Cast off, not too tightly!

Ears (*make 2*)

Cast on 16 stitches with cream yarn.

Knit (K) stitch the first 4 rows.

Change to lilac yarn and Knit (K) stitch for 6 rows.

Cast off.

Fold the ear sections in half and sew up the long side so the back of the ear is cream and the front is lilac, when you reach the top of the ears pull your stitching tightly so it forms a more rounded top to the ear, sew your ends in neatly.

Bow Tie

With green yarn, cast on 7 stitches.

Knit (K) stitch for 16 rows.

Cast off.

Fold the section in half length ways to find the centre, take a needle with green yarn and sew running stitch up the middle, pull tightly and wrap wool round the middle 4 or 5 times to form the middle section of the bow tie.

Making up Mr Rabbit:

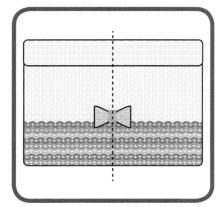

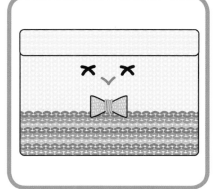

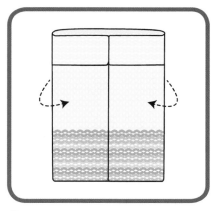

1 Lay the main body section of the rabbit so that the Right Side (the outside) is facing up. Use a ruler to find the centre point of the body, then sew the bow tie neatly in place in the centre just above the lilac stripe.

2 Taking black yarn sew two crosses for the eyes, approx 1 inch/3cm down from the top. Then take lilac yarn and sew a "V" shape for the nose in the centre just below the eyes. Finish sewing off neatly on the inside.

3 Now lay the main body section face up so that the RIGHT side — the nice side — is facing you. Fold inwards from each side, so that the left and right edges meet in the middle. This will be the back of the rabbit.

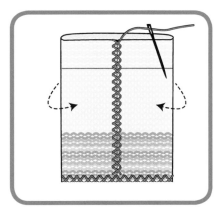

4 Neatly sew the left and right sides together, making sure they meet in the middle of the back of the rabbit. Next sew along the bottom of this section, so that the bottom edges are joined securely too. Turn your Rabbit right sides out now. Almost done!

5 Place each ear inside the top of the body section approx 1/2 inch/1.5cm down, sew neatly in place, hiding the stitches.

EVEN EASIER!

If Mr Rabbit looks a bit too complicated for you, try this simple cosy in 1 colour, knitted in Stocking Stitch (see page 13) in chunky yarn.

Cast on 28 stitches. Knit in Stocking stitch for 34 rows. Cast off and cut yarn leaving a 12 inch/30cm tail. Follow Steps 3 and 4 above to sew together. Sew a loop using ribbon/yarn to the back of the cosy, and a cool button to the front. Make sure the loop fits around the button snuggly enough to hold your device inside the cosy when fastened.

Contributors

I'd like to say a big thanks to the wonderful knitters who contributed some of the wonderful projects in this book:

ADDY WHITFIELD

Addy Whitfield is based in the small Welsh village of Llanfrynach in the Brecon Beacons, where she runs *Gift Horse Kits*, a collection of beginners knitting kits containing all you need to knit a variety of cute creatures. Kits for both the Bunny and Robot projects from this book, containing everything needed to knit each, are available online at **www.gifthorsekits.co.uk**

Project: *Bunny Rabbits, Robot Pals*

ASHLEY HOLDSWORTH

Ashley Holdsworth was taught to knit at the age of six by her granny, and hasn't put her needles down since! She now owns *Make It Glasgow*, a studio in the city centre of Glasgow, Scotland that encourages people to try sewing, dressmaking, knitting, hand-spinning and crochet.
www.makeitglasgow.wordpress.com

Project: *Easy Hat*

IRINA HUBBARD

Irina Hubbard from North Carolina is an Orthodox Christian, wife, mother and professional photographer that loves to knit. Irina taught herself to knit, continuing a family tradition as her Romanian grandmothers were master knitters. You can see her beautiful knitting and photography at **www.purllamb.com**

Project: *Easy i-pod holder*

JENNY McHARDY

Jenny McHardy is a Knitwear Designer based in Aberdeen, Scotland, where she runs her own textile company *Nervous Stitch*, creating beautiful knitted homeware products handmade in Scotland with British lambswool. **www.etsy.com/ shop/nervousstitch**

Project: *Beautiful Bunting, Rabbit i-pod holder*

KATY PENMAN

Katy Penman is a crafter based in Alloa, Scotland and has been knitting for more than 30 years. Katy spent hours as a child designing dolls clothes from odds and ends of wool from her grandmother's projects. Katy now creates and sells eco-friendly, resourceful homewares, accessories and stationery from her online shop **www.girlindustries.etsy.com**

Project: *Fingerless Mittens*

SANDRA FARDON FOX

Sandra Fardon Fox from Oxfordshire, England, returned to knitting about 3 years ago, having originally learned when in the brownies, and loves nothing more than whipping up quick and easy projects and designing her own patterns.

Project: *Pom Pom Scarf*

Models: A big thank you to the beautiful models who posed patiently for the projects in this book — you're all just GORGEOUS! **Bette-Lou, Brodie, Daisy B, Daisy E, Georgia E and Matilda E.**

Learn to Sew: Kids

I hope you've had tons of fun learning to knit. Why not learn to sew with the help of my other books?

Learn To Sew: Kids

My First Hand Sewing Book

The perfect introduction to sewing for beginners. Follow Daisy Doublestitch and Billy Bobbin as they show you how to sew by hand and learn lots of easy stitches and sewing skills. Make super cool projects like Cupcake Pincushions, Crazy Creatures, Birdy Garlands, lovely Love Hearts and more!

Learn To Sew: Kids

Learn to Sew!

Learn how to sew with Daisy Doublestitch and Billy Bobbin, and make some super cool projects, including Kitten Slippers, Cute Cushions, Strawberry Purses, Tissue Monsters and more! Perfect for beginners!

Learn To Sew: Kids

My First Sewing Machine

Get started with your first sewing machine with easy to follow illustrations and instructions! Learn all the parts of a machine and what they do, how to thread your machine and wind your bobbin, how to start and stop sewing, turn corners…AND make your first easy projects — cushions, bags, zip cases, skirts, i-pod cases and more! Sew much fun!

Learn To Sew: Kids

My First Sewing Machine — Fashion School

Calling all budding Fashionistas! If you're just getting started with your sewing machine, and can't wait to make your own cool outfits, then you will LOVE Fashion School! Learn all about making your own clothes, how to recycle your old duds into cool new outfits, and we'll show you how to create some hot new items for your wardrobe — tops, skirts, dresses, lounge pants and more — it's SEW easy!

Printed in Great Britain
by Amazon.co.uk, Ltd.,
Marston Gate.